Knitting projects by Sam Pyle

Published by Top That! Publishing plc
Tide Mill Way, Woodbridge, Suffolk, IP12 1AP, UK
www.topthatpublishing.com

Knitting
Getting Started

Knitting – in case you haven't figured it out yet – happens to be the coolest craft around! Even the celebs are doing it, and you know why? Once you've mastered the basics, you'll find it relaxing, creative and above all fun! Knitting is also great as you don't need loads of expensive special equipment. Most projects just need knitting or crochet needles and wool. Remember to look at the 'you will need' box before each project, as this will tell you what weight and length of wool you need. You can use any colours though!

Needle Know-how

Did you know that everything you'll ever knit is based on the techniques that we will explain here? First, casting on – you need to do this each time you start something new. Then it's just a matter of mastering those 'must-learn' stitches – knit and purl – before casting off. The following instructions apply if you are right-handed.

Casting On

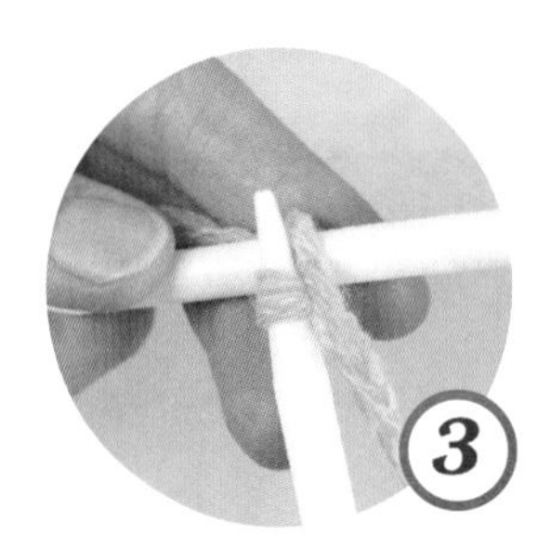

1. Tie your needles together with a loose double knot, leaving a short tail. Hold the tail with your left hand and the wool with your right. Make sure your right needle is behind the left one.

2. Pass the wool over the point of the right-hand needle and under the left, as shown. Slide the wool toward the pointed ends of the needles. Pull the first knot as wide as you can to make a gap.

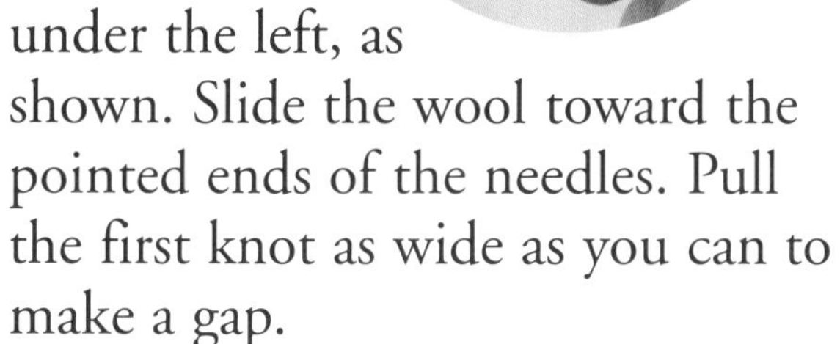

3. Push the tip of the right-hand needle through the gap and take the wool with it.

4. Pull the needles slightly apart. Now use the tip of the left-hand needle to lift this loop off the right-hand needle and onto the left-hand needle. You have cast your first stitch!

5. To cast on your next stitch, insert the tip of the right-hand needle into the top stitch from below and repeat steps 2–4. Keep going until you have cast on the number of stitches that you need.

Knit Stitch

1. Cast on six stitches to start.

2. Hold the needle with the cast-on stitches in your left hand. Hold the tail firmly at the back. Insert the right-hand needle from left to right through the front of the top stitch on the left-hand needle. The right needle should finish behind the left.

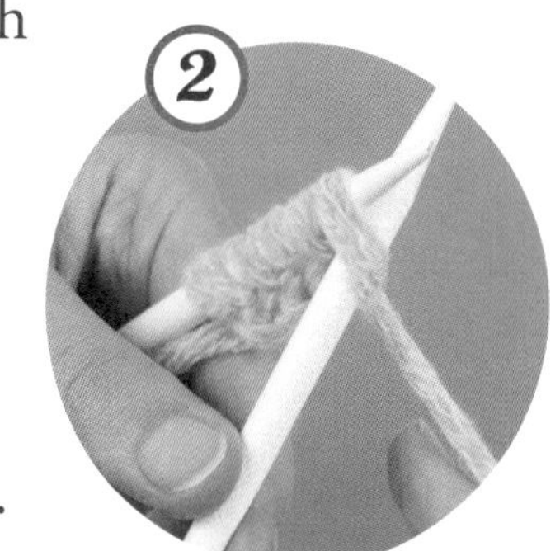

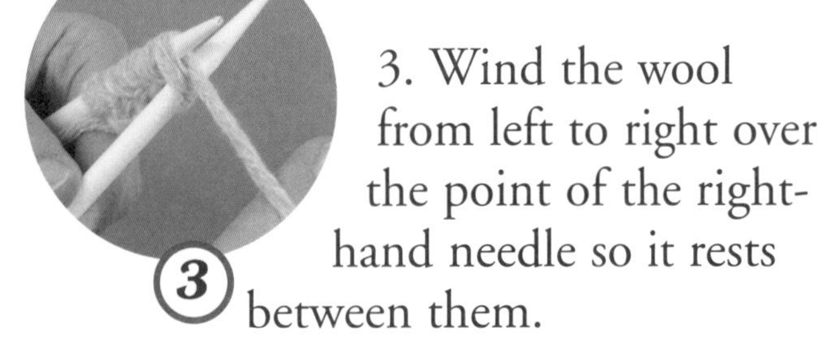

3. Wind the wool from left to right over the point of the right-hand needle so it rests between them.

4. Pull the left-hand needle slightly back from the stitches and move the needles slightly apart to make a gap. Push the tip of the right-hand needle through the loop, bringing the wool with it.

5. A new stitch should have appeared on your right-hand needle. Now 'slip' your original stitch (on the left-hand needle) off its tip. To knit a row, repeat steps 2–5 until you have transferred all of the stitches from your left needle to the right. Then put your empty needle in your right hand, hold the needle with the new stitches in your left and knit another row.

Purl Stitch

1. Make a few knit stitches then bring your wool between the needles and to the front.

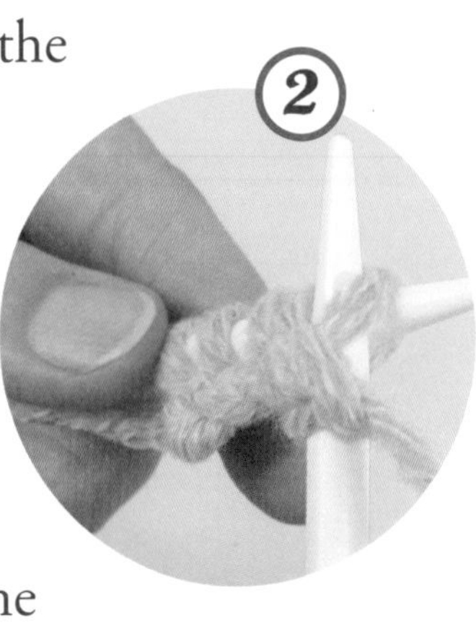

2. Push the tip of the right-hand needle from right to left into the top stitch on the left-hand needle – the right needle should be above the left.

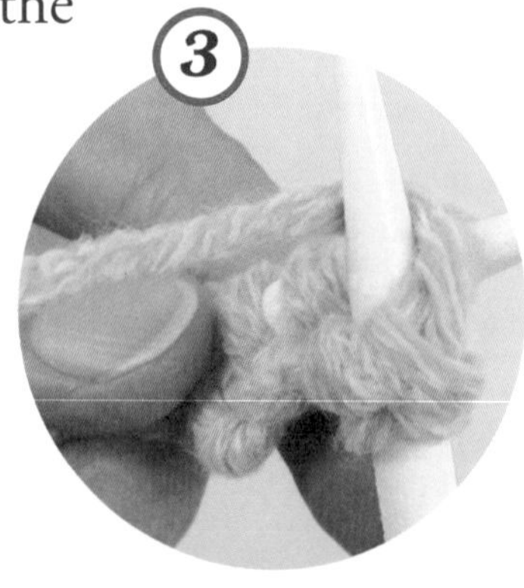

3. Now wind the wool from right to left behind the point of the right-hand needle so that it comes between the needles.

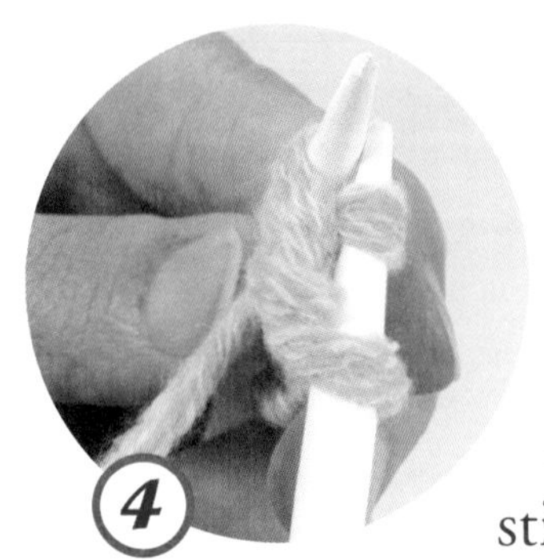

4. Hook the wool back and through the loop, then slip the original stitch off the tip of the left-hand needle just as you did in step 4 for the knit stitch.

5. The first purl stitch will have appeared on your right-hand needle. To keep on purling the row, repeat steps 1–4. Start by inserting the right-hand needle in front of the top stitch on the left-hand needle.

Casting Off

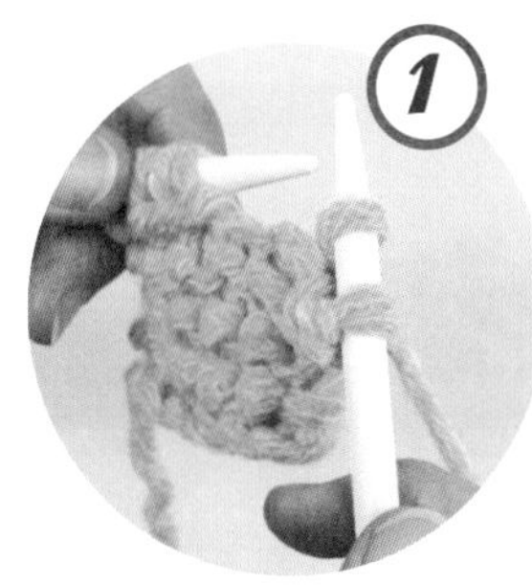

1. Start by knitting two stitches.

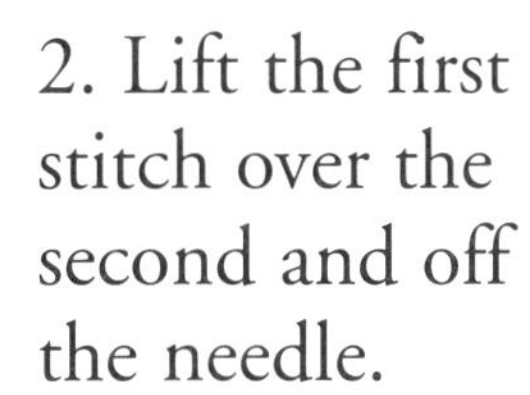

2. Lift the first stitch over the second and off the needle.

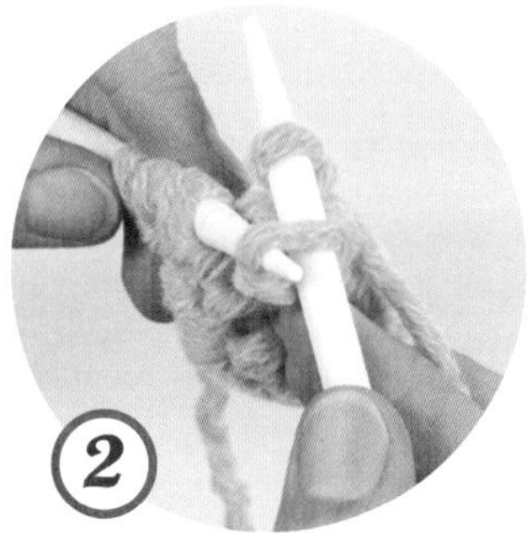

3. This leaves one stitch on the needle. Knit the next stitch as normal so that you have two stitches on the right-hand needle. Then repeat steps 2–3 all the way along the knitted row.

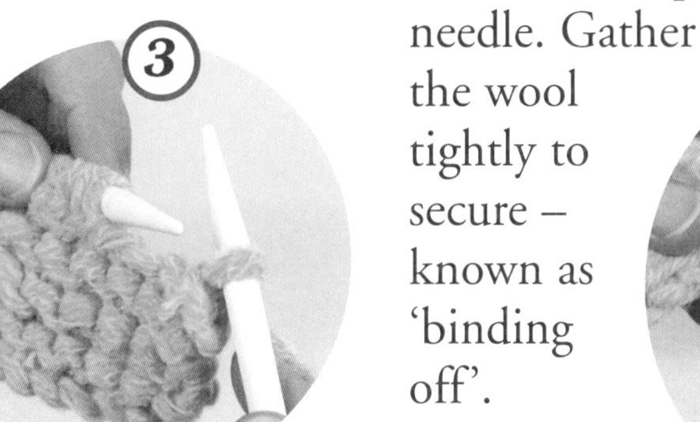

4. Keep going until you have run out of stitches on the left-hand needle and only one remains on the right-hand needle.

5. Thread the tail through the stitch then slip the stitch off the needle. Gather the wool tightly to secure – known as 'binding off'.

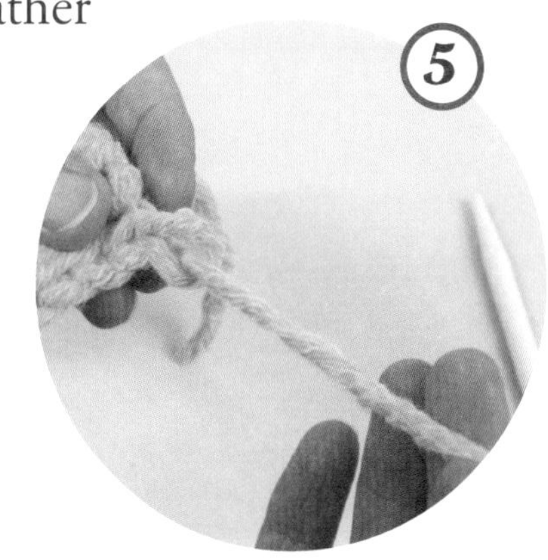

Crochet Chain

1. To crochet a chain you will need a crochet hook. Tie a loose (this is very important) knot around the top of your crochet hook, leaving a short tail, as shown.

2. Hold the hook in your right hand, then holding the tail between your thumb and first finger, bring the wool to wrap around the tip of the hook, as shown.

3. Now bring the wool just in front of the hooked part, as shown.

4. Pull the hook through the original loop, making sure that the part wrapped around in front stays where it is. It will take a while to get the hang of this, as the knotted loop will want to come off too! One stitch will appear above the hook, as shown.

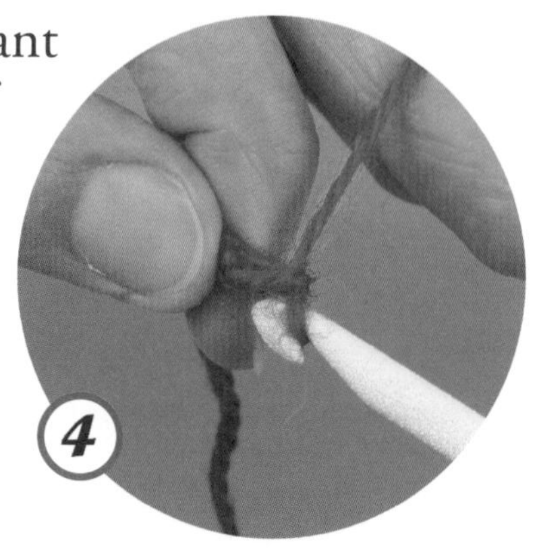

5. To make your next stitch, repeat steps 2–4 and another one will appear on the chain, as shown.

6. Repeat until you have made enough stitches to form a chain of the length you need.

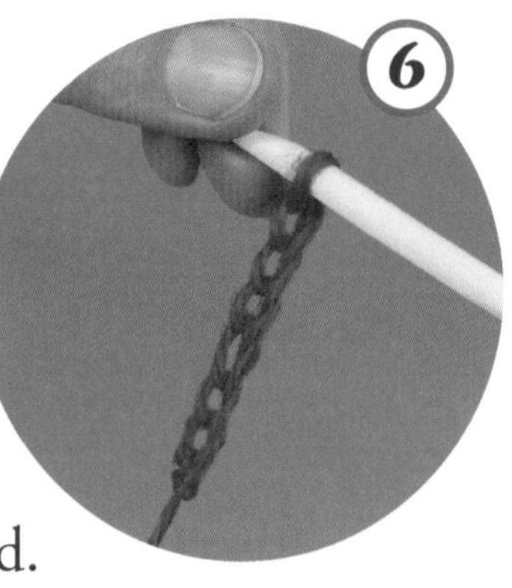

Top Tip: Keep the stitches loose by holding the last chain made between two fingers while you pull the next stitch through. If you don't, you'll have trouble working into these chains later.

Making Pompoms

1. Cut a piece of card the width you want your pompom to be. Hold the end of a ball of wool against the card and start winding it around!

2. Keep going until the wound section is about the same width as the wool shown in the photograph. Then carefully slide the woven section off the card.

3. Cut a long strand of wool (around five times the width of the wound section) and tie it as tightly as you can around the middle of the woven section, as shown. Leave two tails hanging down.

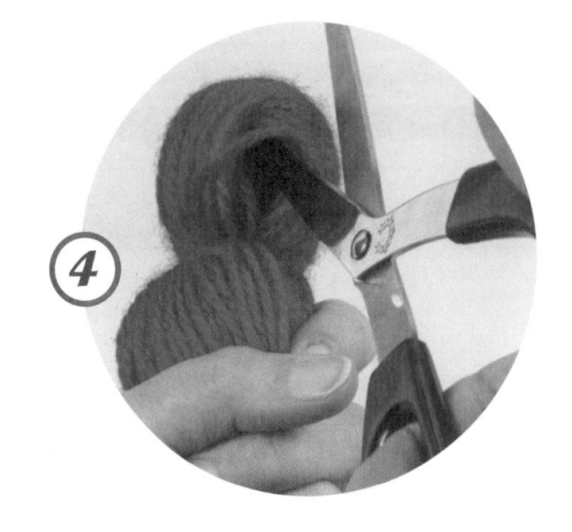

4. By tying the middle, you will have created loops at either end of the wound section. Insert the tip of your scissors into one of the loops and cut through the wool, as shown above.

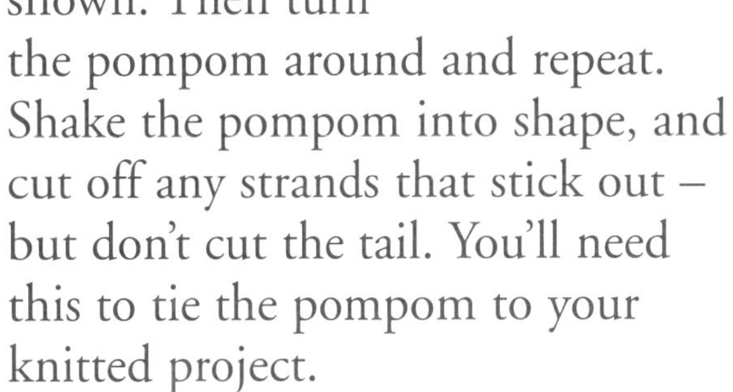

5. Once you have snipped all the way through the first loop, fan out the ends, as shown. Then turn the pompom around and repeat. Shake the pompom into shape, and cut off any strands that stick out – but don't cut the tail. You'll need this to tie the pompom to your knitted project.

Cool Clutch Bag

1. Cast on 30 stitches and knit 70 rows until you have a rectangular shape, as shown.

2. To make the two sloping sides of the flap, you need to knit two stitches together (we will now refer to this as 'K2tog'). Insert the right needle into the first two stitches on the left needle and knit two like this. Then knit as normal to the end of the row until you have two stitches left, then 'K2tog' again. Repeat until there are four stitches left, then cast off.

Here you'll learn how to create a pointed edge to your knitting. This gorgeous going-out bag takes around three hours to make.

YOU WILL NEED:

- 1 skein of pure wool: 100 g (3 ½ oz) / 160 m (174 yards) / no.5 bulky - must not be machine washable – very important!
- wool needle
- ribbon 25 cm / 10 inches long
- beads
- a sewing needle

3. Thread your wool needle with a spare piece of wool and fold the bottom section up, as shown. Stitch the sides together to make an 'envelope'.

4. Fill a bowl with warm water and washing-up liquid. Put your bag in and start moving it around.

5. Keep washing and rubbing until the wool goes stiff and shrinks to a suitable bag size. Pull into shape and dry flat.

6. Sew one piece of ribbon to the point of the flap and one underneath and tie.

7. Then stitch on your beads to finish.

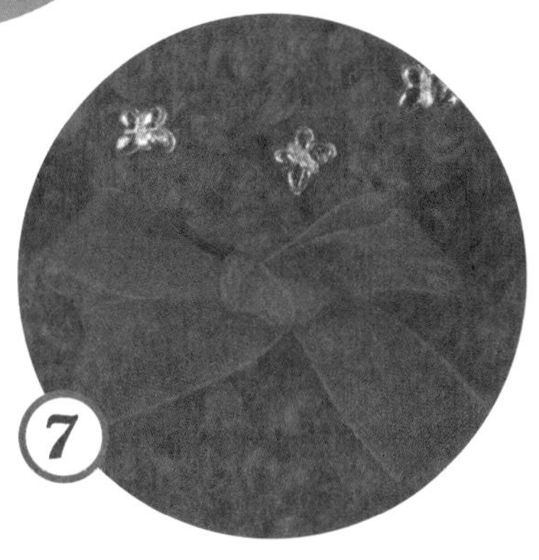

MP3 Sock

This project uses knit and purl stitches and takes around two hours to complete.

YOU WILL NEED:

- ½ skein silky wool: 50 g (1 ¾ oz) / 95 m (104 yards) / no.3
- wool needle
- a ruler

1. For a MP3 player 6 cm wide, cast on 20 stitches and knit 32 rows, as shown above. If your player is narrower, see the box on page 11 and knit until the section is long enough.

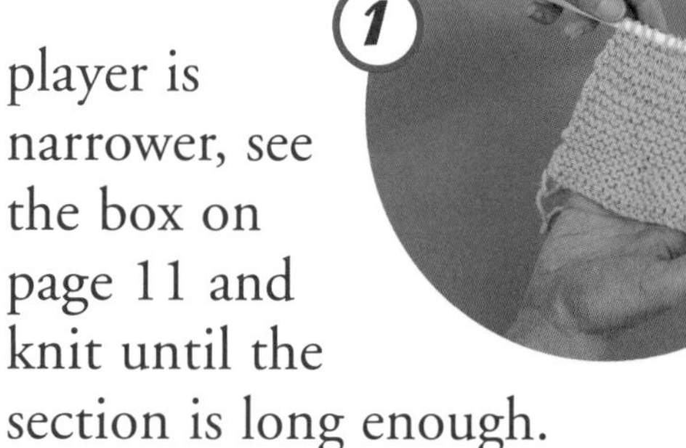

2. Create that cool ribbed effect below at the top of the cover by firstly knitting two stitches, then bringing the wool forward. Purl two stitches (see pages 4– 5), then take the wool back. Repeat until the end of the row, then turn around and do the same when coming back. Repeat for six more rows, then cast off, leaving a 46 cm tail.

3. Place your knitted section with the 'wrong' side facedown and fold in half lengthwise.

4. To sew up; thread the wool needle with the tail. Then insert the needle through the first knitted stitch. Pull the wool through and carry it over the top of the sock.

4

Insert the needle into the next knitted stitch and repeat. Start at the top edge, work along the long side, and finish at the bottom edge. Tie a knot to secure.

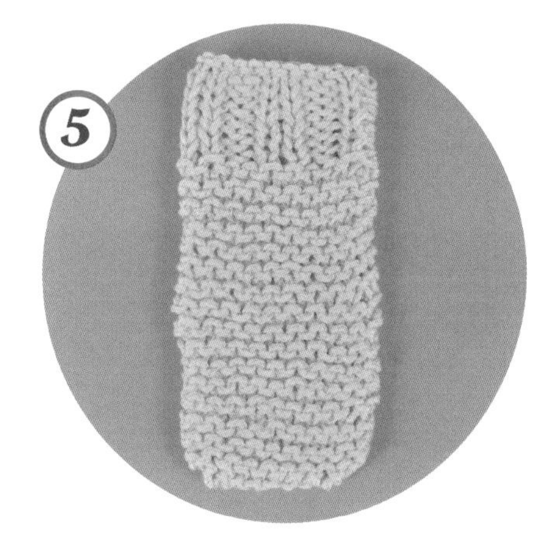

5. Turn the sock the right way around, and fold down the ribbed edge. Put your MP3 player into its sock and it'll stay safe from scratches!

Top Tip: This project fits an MP3 player measuring 6 cm wide. Cast on the following amount of stitches for players of the following widths:

4 cm = 12 stitches
2 1/2 cm = 8 stitches

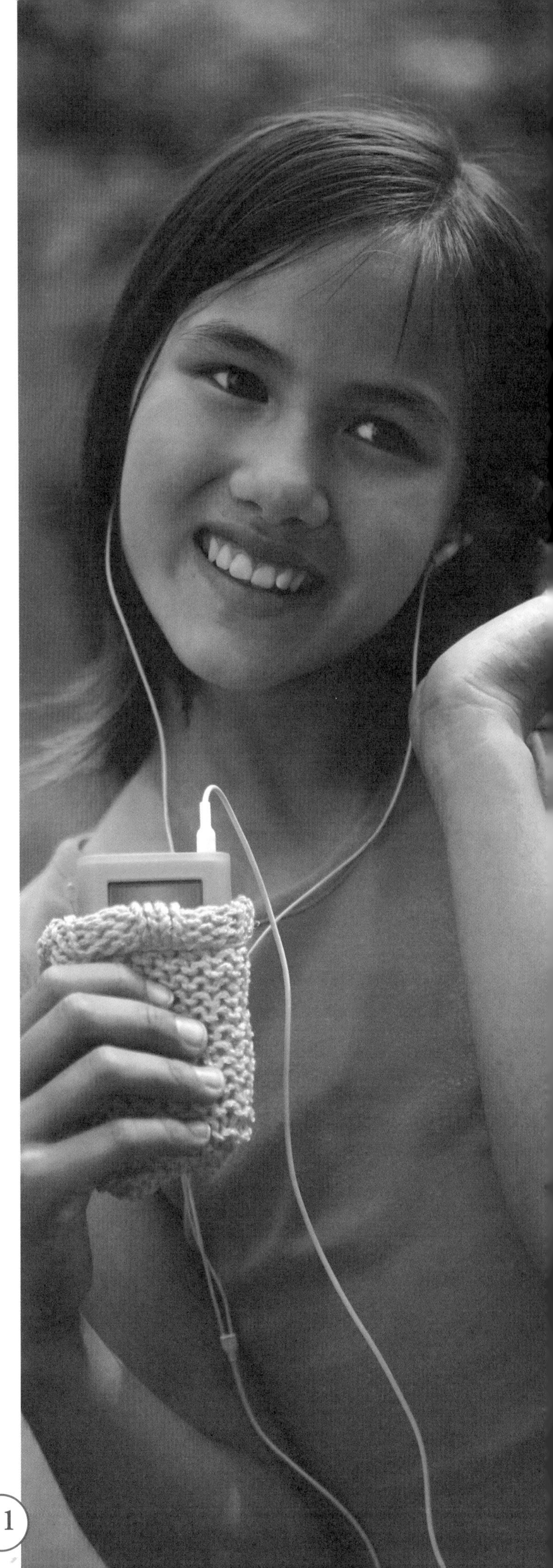

Pretty Poncho

This warm poncho uses lots of basic knit stitches. Allow yourself a day to do this one – the result will be worth it!

YOU WILL NEED:

- 1 skein chunky wool no.4
- 1 skein 'rag' wool no.3
- 1 skein plain wool no.3
  all 100 g (3 ½ oz) / 280 m (306 yards)
- wool needle

1. Cast on 40 stitches of your chunky wool and knit 80 rows. Then hold the cast-on row from your shoulder to elbow to see how far the knitted section comes down. Stop knitting if it's long enough, or keep going until it reaches to your waist. You should end up with a large rectangle, as shown. Don't cast off, but leave your wool to one side. Hang on to your needles!

1

2. Now it's time to change your wool. Pick up the plain and rag wool and continue to knit as normal but holding these two together. You can see the two separate strands in the photo, above. Since the rag wool is thin, knitting it together with a thicker plain wool means that the knitting will be stronger.

2

3. Keep knitting the two wools together until the rows are as wide as your shoulder. Now cast off.

4. Now repeat steps 1–4 with the remaining wool to create an identical knitted section. Lay them out, as shown.

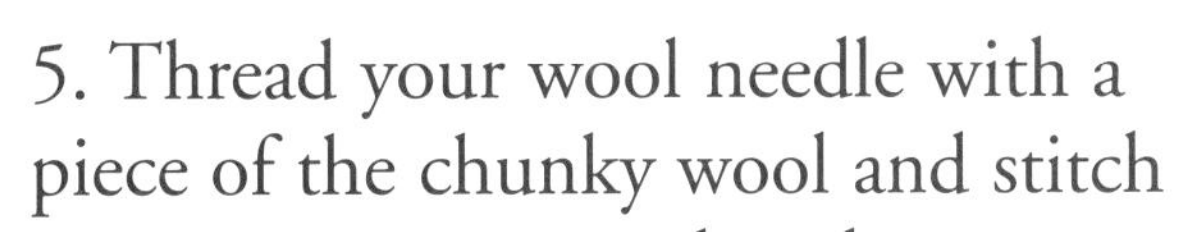

5. Thread your wool needle with a piece of the chunky wool and stitch together the two short edges to the two long edges. Open out and place the gap over your head. There you go – a beautiful warm poncho!

Top Tip: To see if your needles are long enough, hold the tip of one of your needles against your ear. The length of the needle is how wide the poncho will be. If you need it to be wider, use longer needles.

Ribbon Pouch

No knitting, all crochet! Remember to keep your stitches nice and loose. Allow five hours to complete.

YOU WILL NEED:

- 1 skein plain or 'hairy' wool 50 g (1 ¾ oz) / 60 m (66 yards) / no.4
- crochet hook
- 42 in. / 1.6 m / ribbon

1. Tie a loose loop around the hook. Hold the chain at the knot, and make a chain of two stitches (see page 6 for instructions on crocheting a chain).

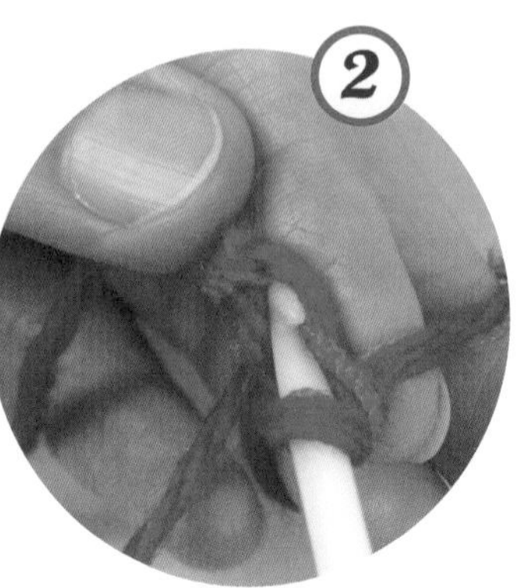

2. To make the base; put the hook into the first loop – the one with the knot.

3. Hook the wool around, and pull through. You should have two loops left.

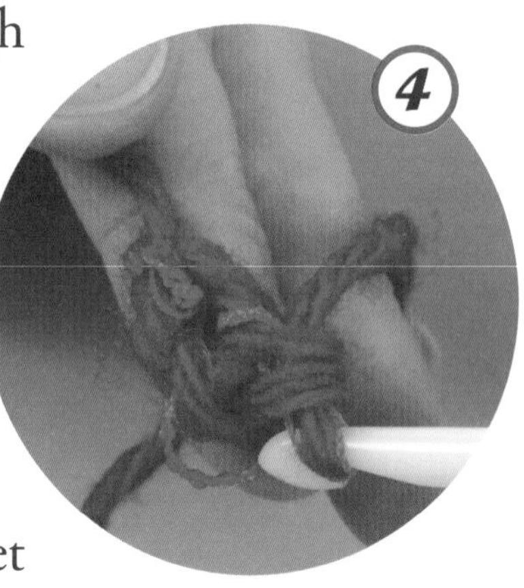

4. Hook up the wool again and draw through both loops. You now have one loop on the hook. This is known as a single crochet stitch.

5. Repeat steps 2–3 five times. You will end up with six single crochet stitches around the original loop.

6. To complete the first round, put the hook through the first chain stitch you made.

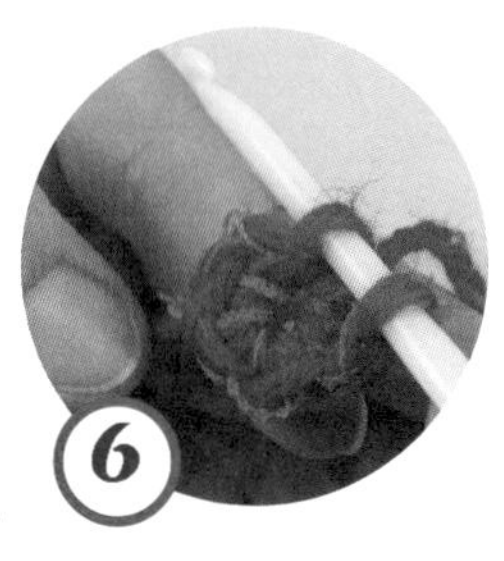

7. Hook the wool and pull through the chain and original loop together. This makes a slip stitch.

8. You have completed the first round. Now make two more chains.

9. Then, make two single crochet stitches into each of the original six stitches. Join the first to the last by slip stitching again.

10. Repeat for the next round, and you will finish with a ring of 24 stitches.

11. For the last round, finish by crocheting one single stitch into the first, but two in the second, then one in the third, two in the fourth and alternate until you have finished a ring of 36 stitches. Slip stitch to finish. You will end up with a round base, as shown.

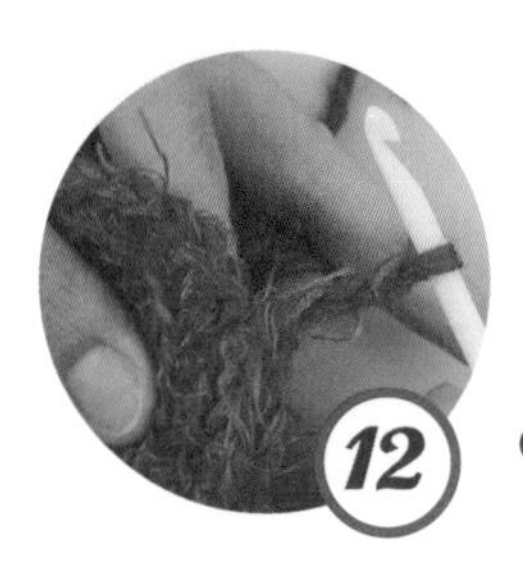

12. To make the sides; first, crochet a chain of three.

13. Now wrap the wool once around the hook before you put it into the next stitch.

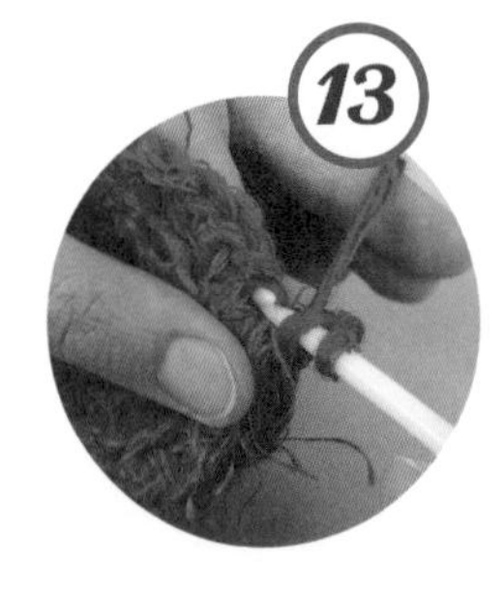

14. Hook up the wool and draw it back through – you should have three loops on the hook.

15. Hook up the wool again and draw through two loops – you should still have two loops.

16. Hook the wool around again and draw through two loops to leave one – this is a double crochet stitch.

17. Repeat the double crochet stitches into each stitch in your base. When you get back to the start, join the first and last stitches by slip stitching into the second chain.

18. Now repeat from the chain of three to make the next row around the sides. Keep going until the sides are high enough to make a bag.

19. At the end of the last row, cut the wool 5 cm from the hook, make a slip stitch, pull the tail through the last loop and pull tight. You should have the basic nest shape.

20. Stitch the loose end down on the inside of the bag using the wool needle.

21. Around 1½ cm from the top of the bag, weave the ribbon in and out of the loose holes formed by your crocheting. Pull the ribbon gently to gather up the sides of the bag, and tie.

Top Tip: **Since this project is the most intricate, we have used a plain wool in the photos to make the steps clear. Once you're confident, you might like to use a 'hairy' wool as in the finished photo on page 15!**

Creative Bracelets
Getting Started

Want to show someone you care? Then why not give them a friendship bracelet!

The following pages will teach you how to make amazing friendship bracelets, simply by following the illustrated step-by-step instructions.

We've used colourful threads in the prettiest shades of blue, purple and pink to make our bracelet designs. At the beginning of each design, you'll see how much thread you need and the colours to use. You can follow our suggestions, or you can design your own colour combinations using your favourite colours. Thread to make the bracelets can be bought easily and cheaply from sewing or hobby shops, where you'll be able to buy embroidery thread in all the colours of the rainbow!

Remember that you don't have to stick to threads – you can use other materials to add your own touch. Thin string and leather cord make cool, chunky-looking bracelets, while silver and gold wool can be woven through plain colours for a glittery effect. You can also add beautiful beads - simply tie them to the ends or weave them into the designs. You might want to buy a needle threader to help thread the beads.

EASY WEAVING

It's very important to keep the threads separate while you're making your bracelets. You can make an easy weaving card by using a piece of card with a bulldog clip at the top or use a clipboard.

To use a weaving card, cut the threads to the lengths in the instructions and tie them together at one end. Unless the instructions tell you differently, leave about 5 cm between the ends and the knot. Place the ends under the clip and get braiding!

PLAITING

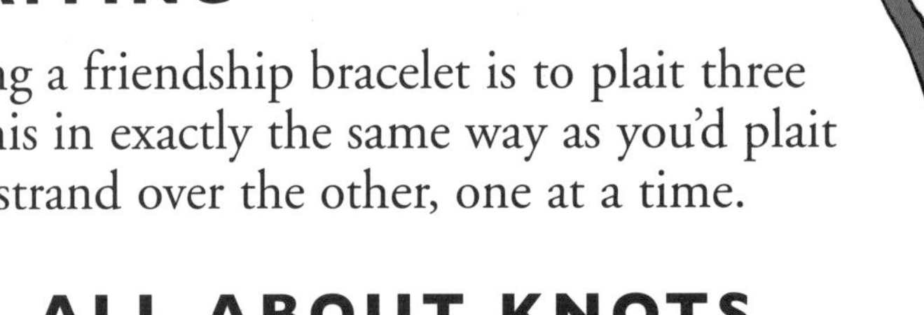

The simplest way of making a friendship bracelet is to plait three threads together. You do this in exactly the same way as you'd plait your hair, by crossing one strand over the other, one at a time.

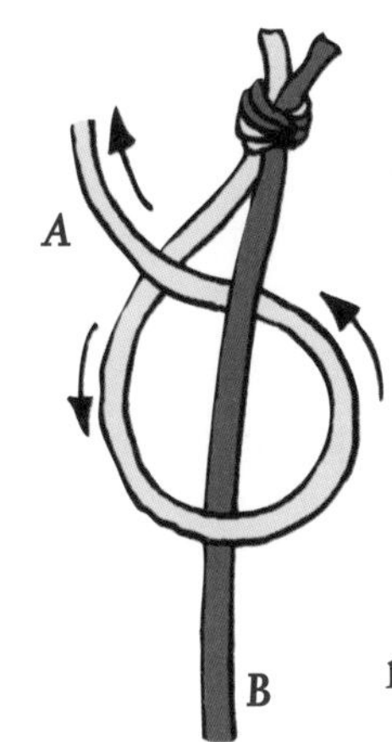

ALL ABOUT KNOTS

The most important knot in the book is the basic 'friendship knot'. Getting the tension right is essential if you want to make successful friendship bracelets, so practise this before you start the bracelet projects.

1. Start with two pieces of thread which you have tied together. Hold thread B firmly in one hand, and pass thread A over thread B, making a loop, as shown.

2. Tuck thread A back under B, and up through the loop.

3. Pull the threads gently, so that the knot is pushed right up to the starting knot.

And that's how to tie a friendship knot!

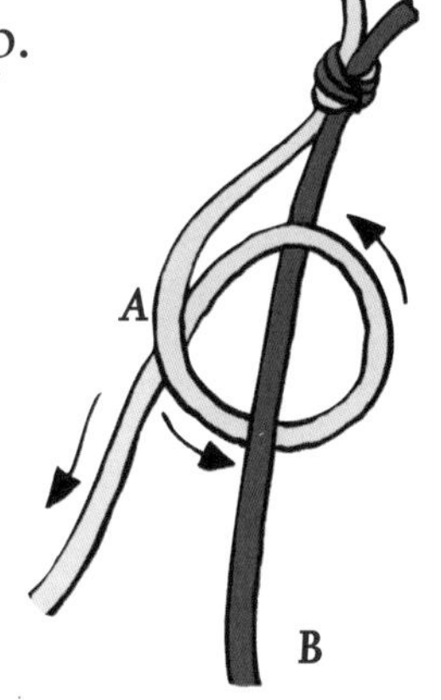

REVERSE KNOT

To make a reverse knot, pass thread A under thread B, then back over and down through the loop.

STARTING AND FINISHING

To tie the threads together at the start of each project, use a knot, as shown left.

Once the bracelet is long enough to go around your wrist, tie the loose ends together with the same type of knot you used at the beginning. Cut the threads, allowing an extra 5 cm after the knot.

WEARING YOUR BRACELET

Finally, use this kind of knot to tie the loose ends around your wrist.

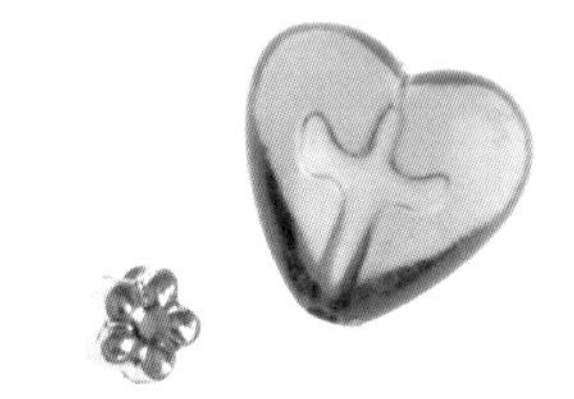

Loop the Loop

Colours: Lilac, purple
Length: Lilac: two 54 cm lengths; purple: two 30 cm lengths
Beads: Six silver star beads

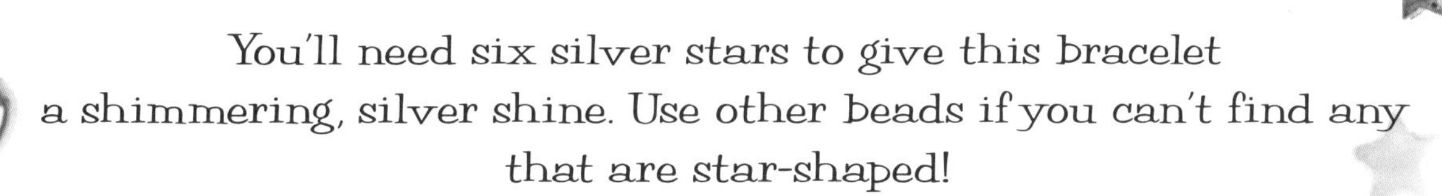

You'll need six silver stars to give this bracelet a shimmering, silver shine. Use other beads if you can't find any that are star-shaped!

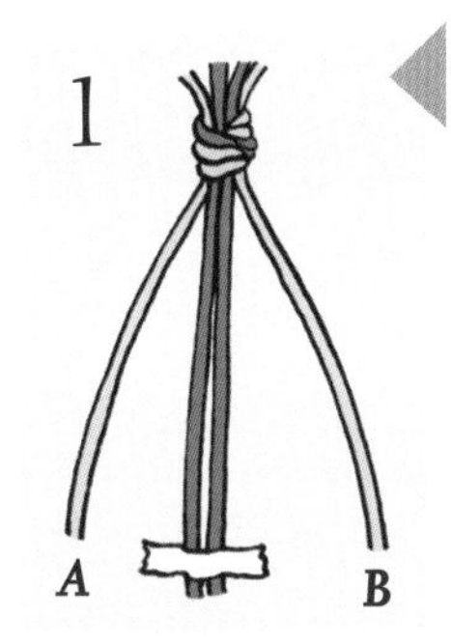

1. Tie the threads together and separate them over the weaving card. Keep the purple threads straight by taping the ends to the weaving card.

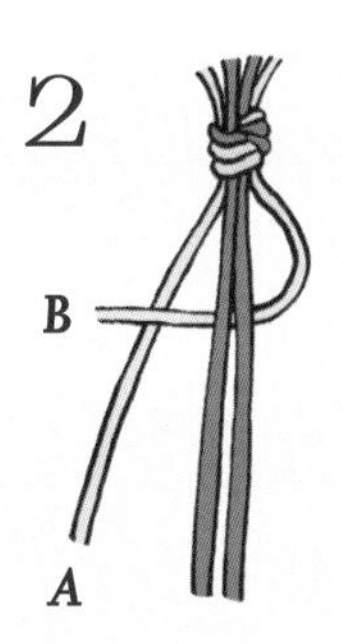

2. Pass lilac thread B under the purple threads and over lilac thread A.

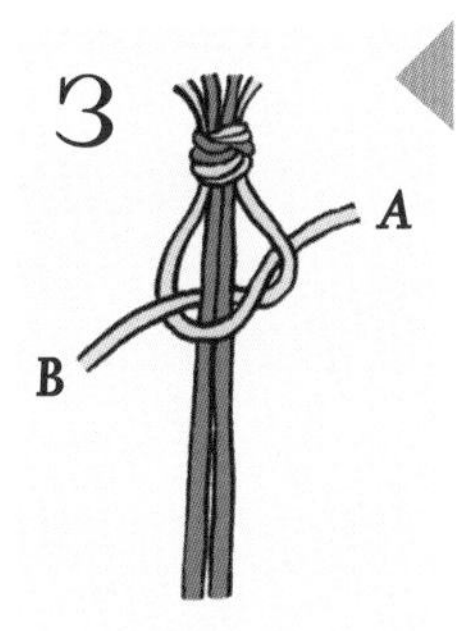

3. Pass lilac thread A over the purple threads and under lilac thread B. Pull both of the lilac threads gently, so that the loop moves towards the knot.

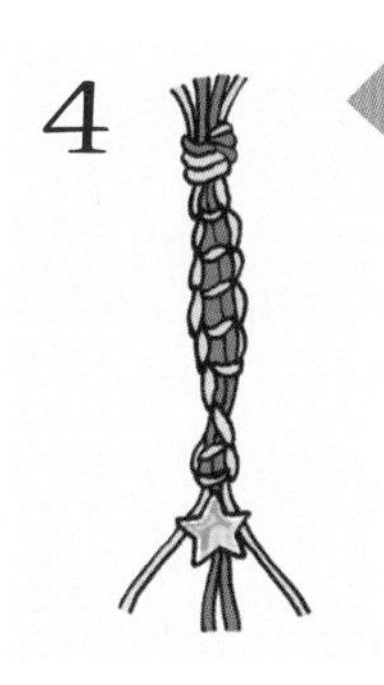

4. Repeat steps 2 and 3 eight times, starting each loop with the right-hand thread. Slip a star bead onto the purple threads. Repeat steps 2–4 five more times, then finish as usual.

Make an extra-special bracelet by tying three together! Make three Loop the Loop designs in your favourite colours, adding beads if you want, and then tie them all together!

Friendly Foursome

Colours: Black, maroon, dark blue, pale blue
Length: Two 30 cm lengths of each colour

This plait uses four double strands to make a more complicated plait.

1. Tie the threads together and secure on your weaving card.

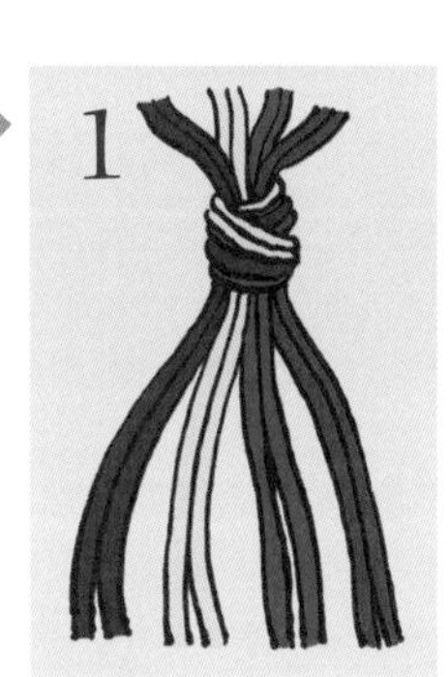

2. Put the black threads over the pale blue, then take them under the dark blue and over the maroon. Tug the black threads gently, so that they are pulled up to the starting knot.

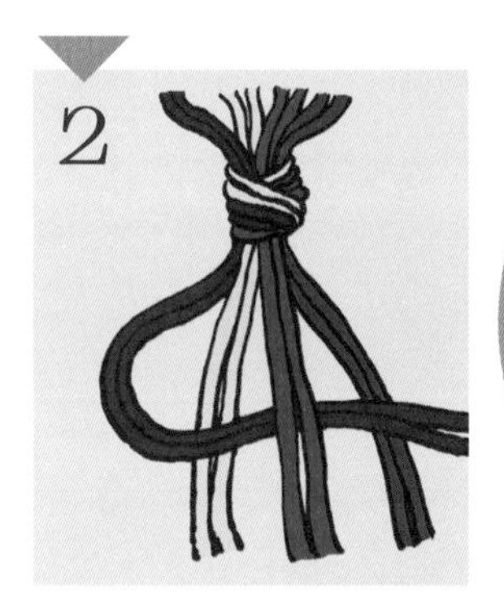

You can use five, six, seven or eight double threads to make an even wider band! Just keep weaving the threads over and under the ones to the right.

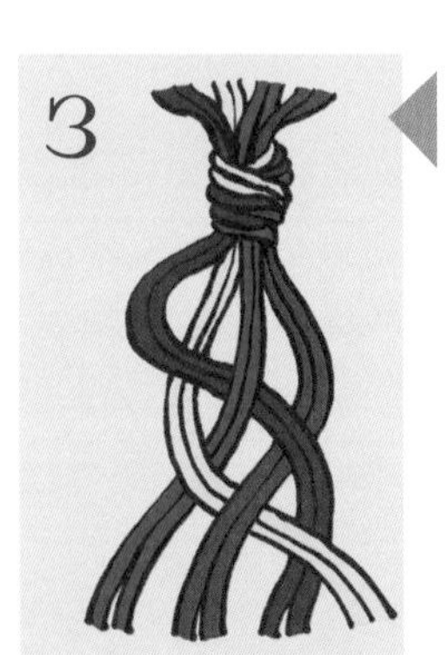

3. Repeat with the pale blue, dark blue and maroon threads.

4. Keep going until the plait is long enough to go around your wrist, then tie the ends in the usual way.

Create an anklet by following the *Friendly Foursome* design, this time using four lengths of each colour rather than two. Keep plaiting until the band is long enough to fit comfortably around your ankle, then tie the ends in the usual way. Use a needle and thread to sew a big bead onto the middle for a glamorous finishing touch!

Pretty in Pink

Colours: Purple, pink
Length: Purple: one 120 cm length; pink: two 30 cm lengths

With this bracelet, the longer purple thread weaves in and out of the shorter pink ones.

1. Tie the threads and fix them onto the weaving card. Pass the purple thread over pink thread B, and then under pink thread A.

2. Then bring it back over pink A, and under pink B.

3. Tug the threads gently, so that the loop slides up near the starting knot.

4. Repeat steps 2 and 3, weaving the purple thread around the pink.

5. Stop weaving once it is long enough to fit your wrist. Tie the loose ends together as usual.

Beautiful Beads

Once you've mastered the basic method shown above, why not try weaving beads into the bracelet?

Tie the threads and fix them onto the weaving card. Slip a bead onto the purple thread and tie a knot. Follow steps 2 and 3 above, until your bracelet is about 3 cm long. Weave three more 3 cm sections, threading a bead onto the end of each, then knot the ends as usual.

Star Bright

Colours: Lilac, pale blue, dark blue
Length: Lilac and pale blue: one 28 cm length; dark blue: two 28 cm lengths
Beads: Four white star beads

You'll need four white star beads to make this star-spangled design.

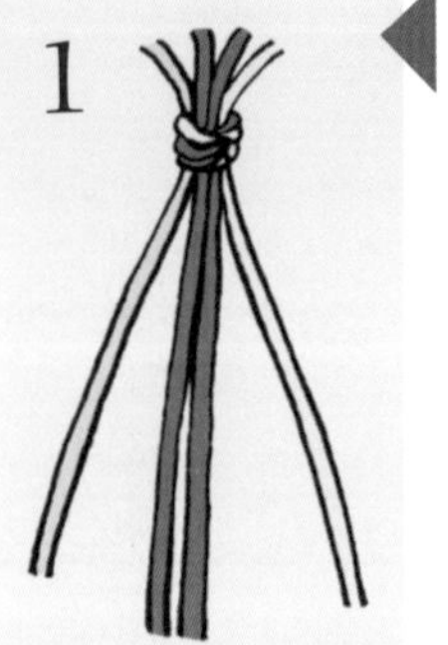

1. Tie the four threads together, and separate them out on the weaving card, as shown.

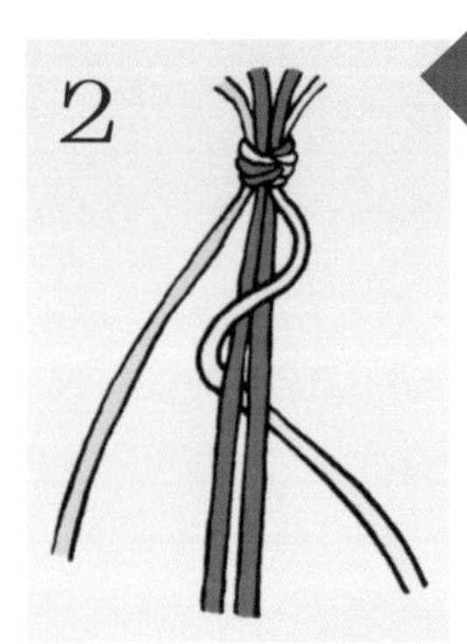

2. Take the pale blue thread over the dark blue threads, then pass it underneath the dark blue threads and return it to its original position.

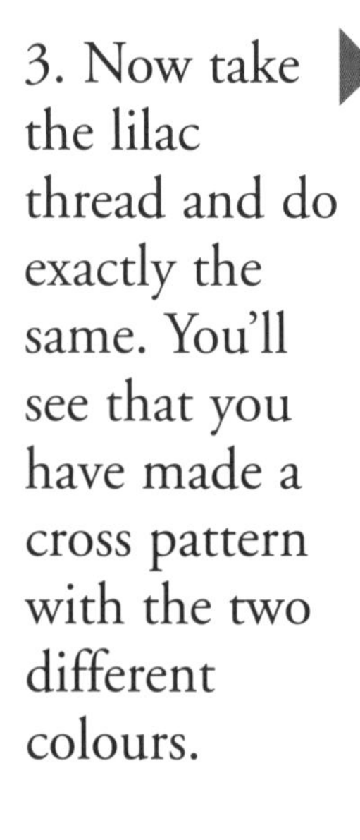

3. Now take the lilac thread and do exactly the same. You'll see that you have made a cross pattern with the two different colours.

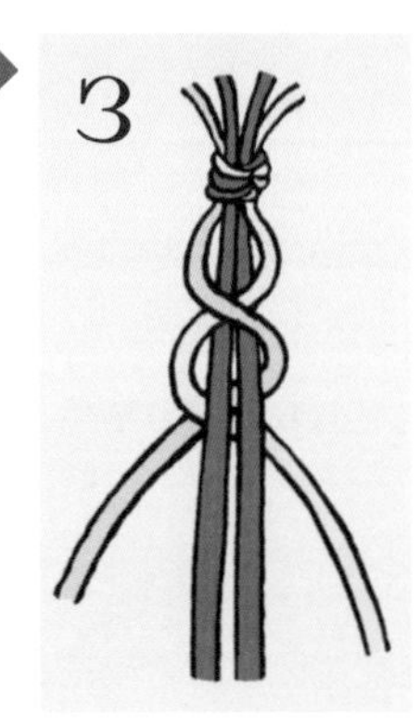

4. Repeat steps 2 and 3 for about 2 cm, then thread one of the star beads onto the dark blue threads.

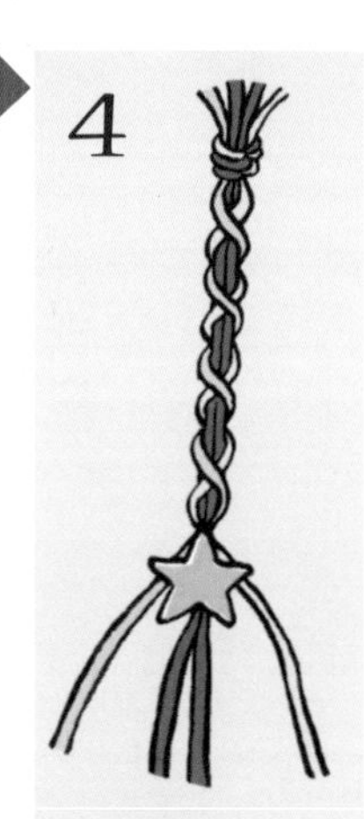

5. Repeat steps 2–4 three more times, finishing the bracelet with 2 cm of cross pattern and a knot to tie the loose ends together.

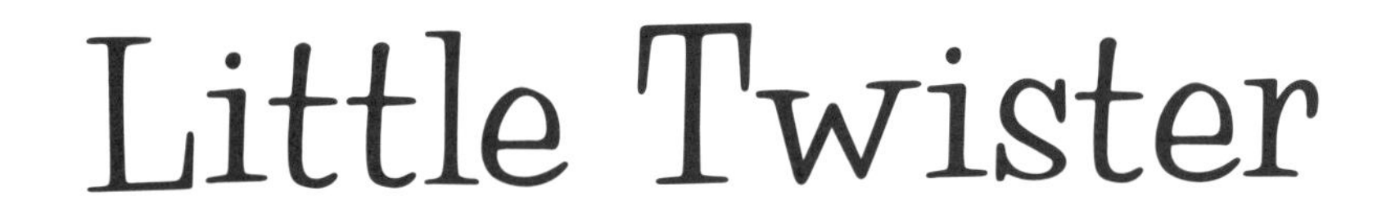

Little Twister

Colours: Purple, maroon, pale blue, lilac, dark blue, violet
Length: One 60 cm length of each colour
Beads: One large silver bead

This is the only bracelet that's made just by twisting!

1. Tie the threads together in a knot at one end. You won't need the weaving card for this bracelet – just tape the knot firmly to a work surface.

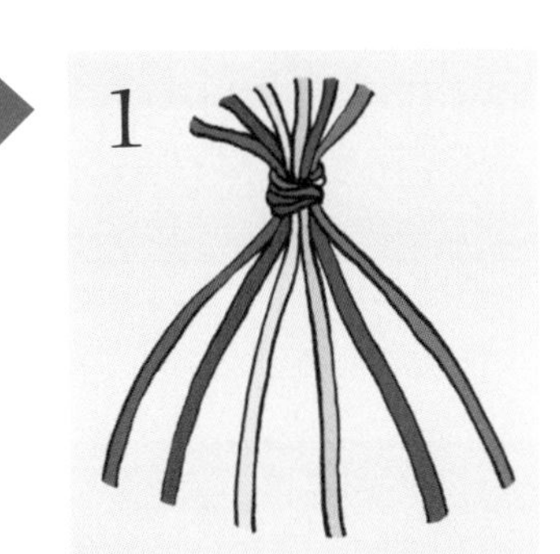

2. Twist all the threads tightly together in the same direction.

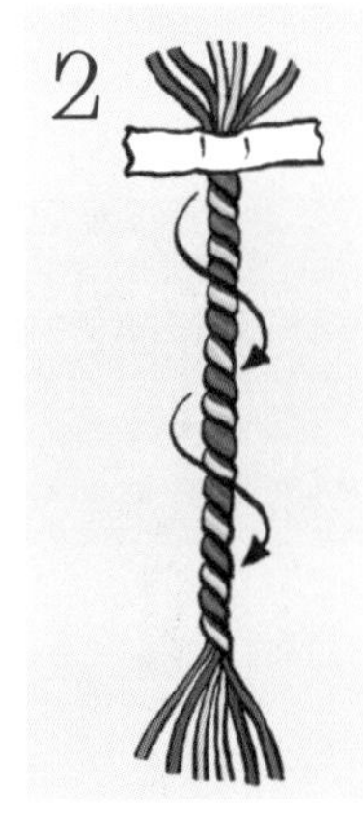

3. Bend the twisted threads in half, so that they twist around themselves.

4. Tie the loose ends together, then thread on a large silver bead. Tie another knot immediately after the bead. To fix your *Little Twister* around your wrist, all you have to do is pull the bead through the loop at the other end of the bracelet!

Round and Round

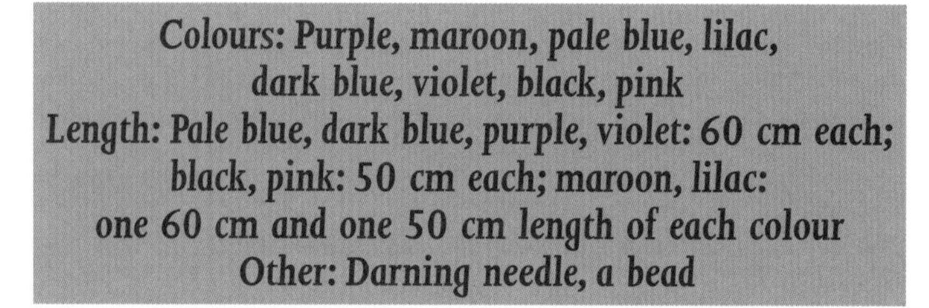
Colours: Purple, maroon, pale blue, lilac, dark blue, violet, black, pink
Length: Pale blue, dark blue, purple, violet: 60 cm each; black, pink: 50 cm each; maroon, lilac: one 60 cm and one 50 cm length of each colour
Other: Darning needle, a bead

This one's a real smoothie! As well as all your threads, you'll also need a darning needle and a bead.

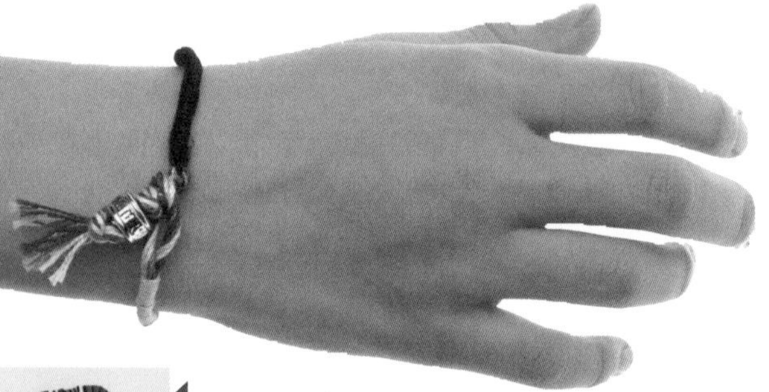

1. Make the *Little Twister* (page 23) using all the 60 cm lengths of thread.

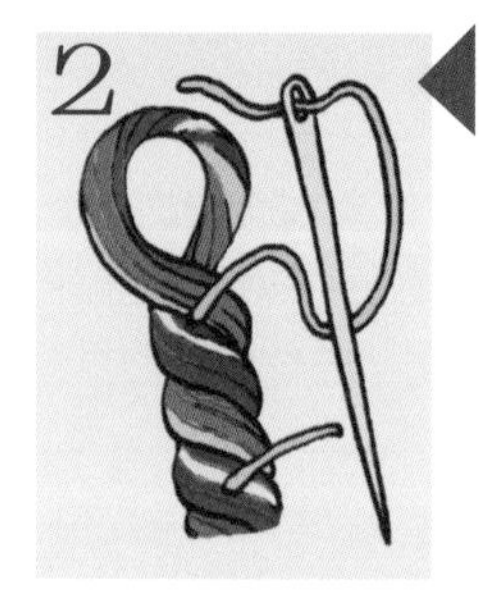

2. Thread a needle with one 50 cm length of thread. Push the needle into the bracelet about 2 cm away from the looped end, and pull the thread through. Leave a tiny piece of the loose end showing.

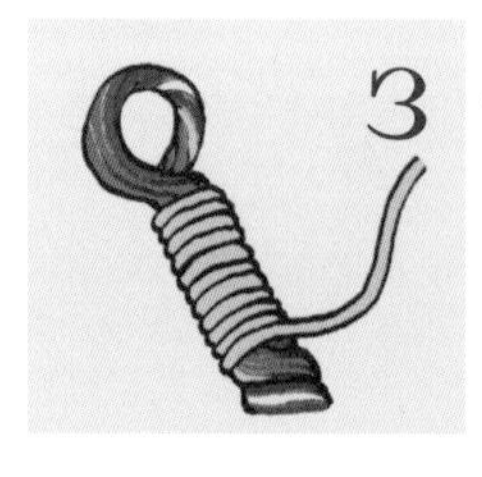

3. Take the thread off the needle and wind it tightly around, covering the bracelet beneath and the loose end as you go.

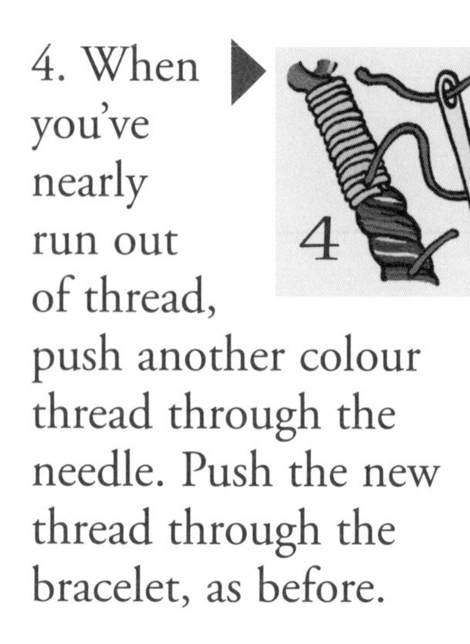

4. When you've nearly run out of thread, push another colour thread through the needle. Push the new thread through the bracelet, as before.

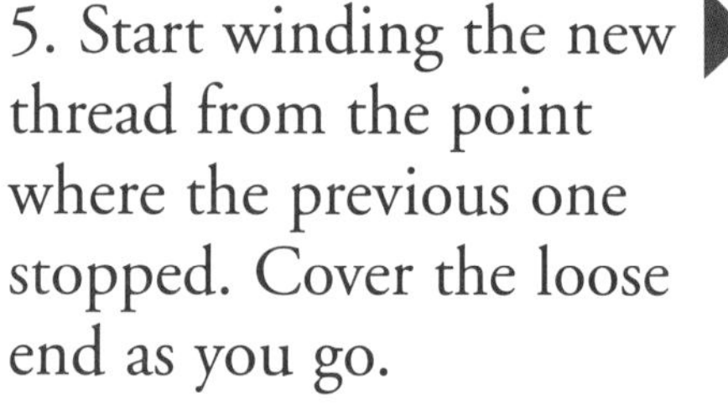

5. Start winding the new thread from the point where the previous one stopped. Cover the loose end as you go.

6. Carry on winding the coloured threads around until you've covered the whole bracelet. Use the needle to tuck in the last loose end. Tie the bead on the end of the bracelet.

Cool Chevron

Colours: Purple, violet, lilac
Length: Two 70 cm lengths of each colour

This classy-looking bracelet gets you knotting from both directions!

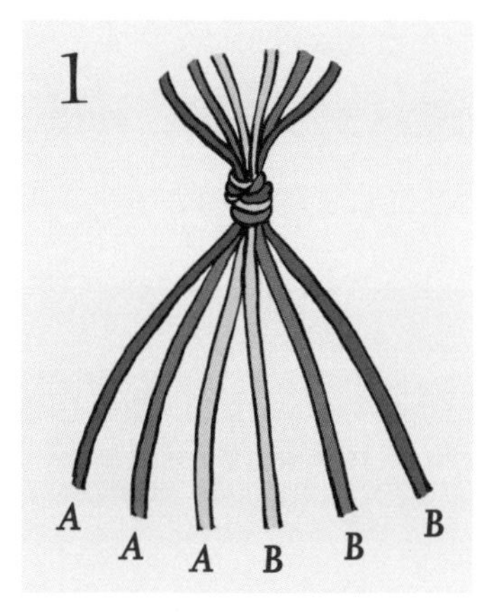

1. Tie the threads and fix them to the weaving card, as shown left.

2. Take the purple thread A. Make two friendship knots over violet A and lilac A (see page 18).

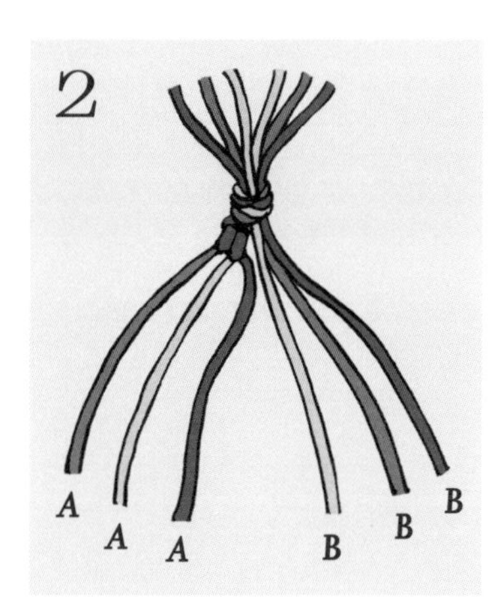

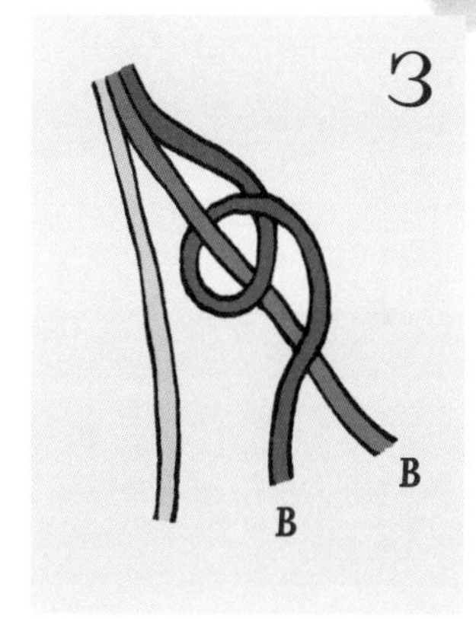

3. Take purple thread B, and make one friendship knot on violet thread B.

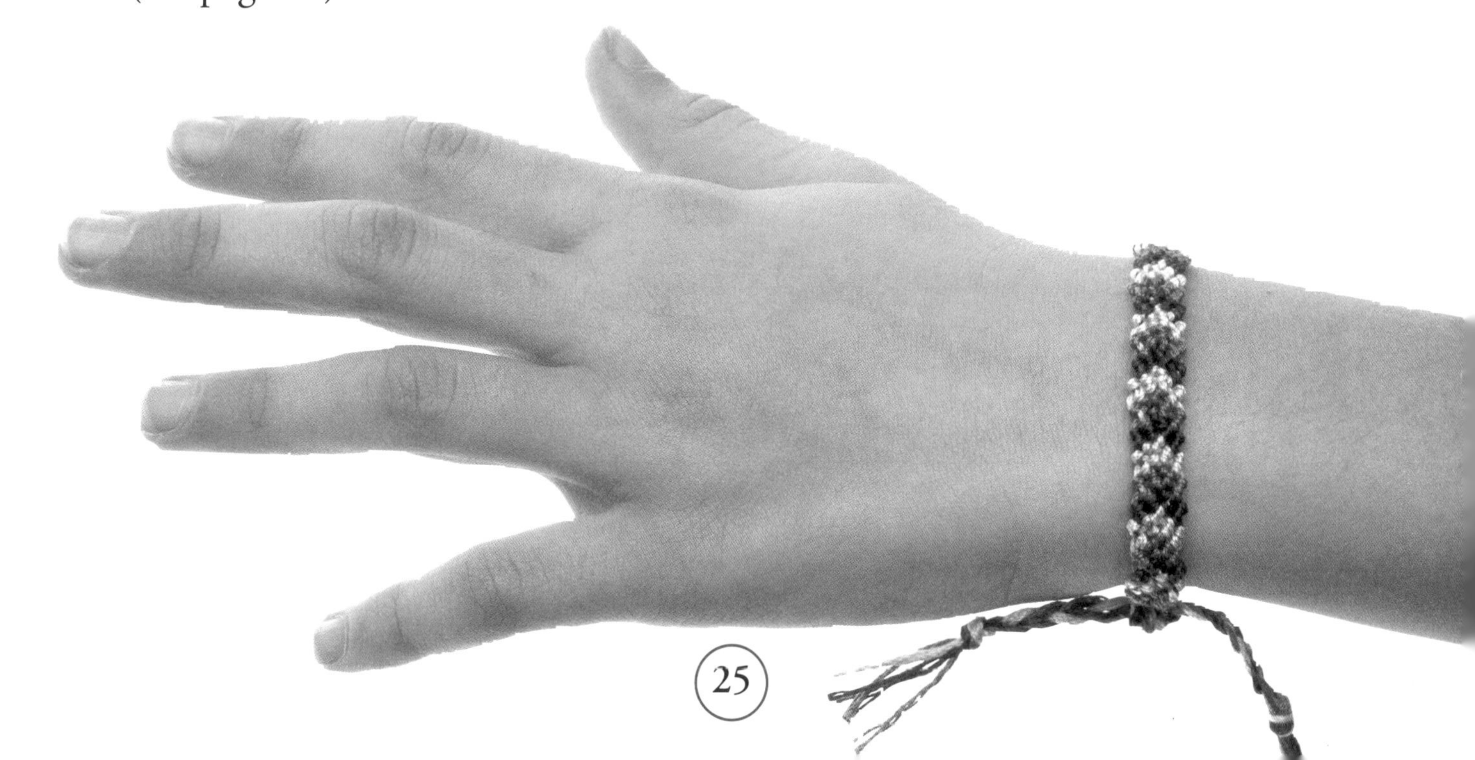

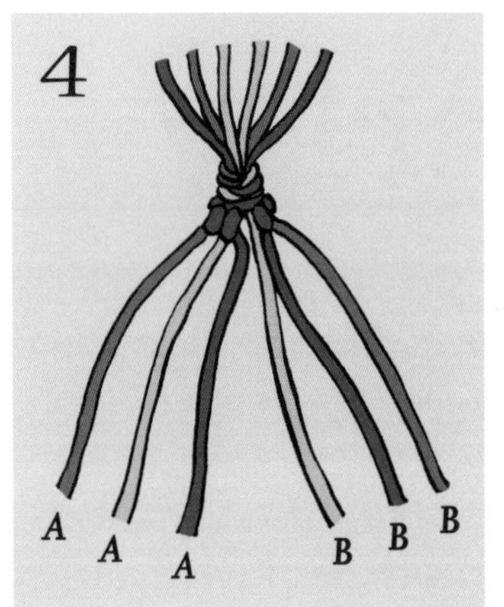

4. Then use purple B to make a reverse knot on violet thread B. Tighten the knot, and push it up to the top.

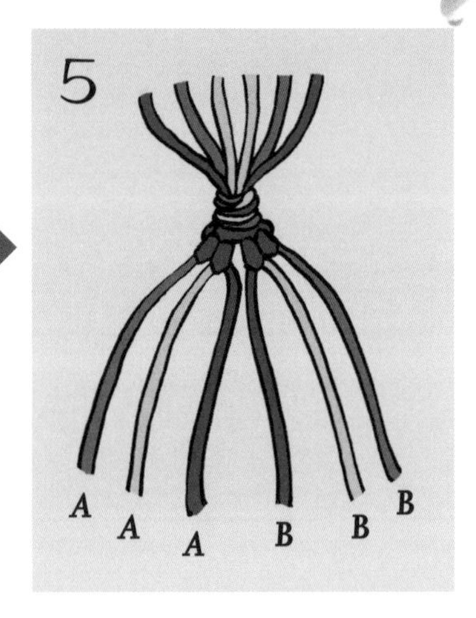

5. Now use purple B to make identical knots on lilac B.

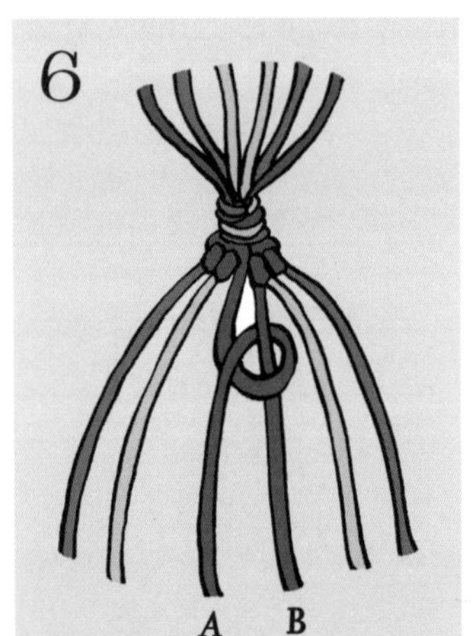

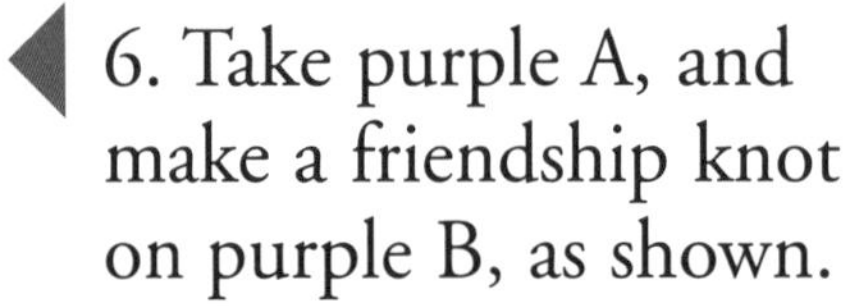

6. Take purple A, and make a friendship knot on purple B, as shown.

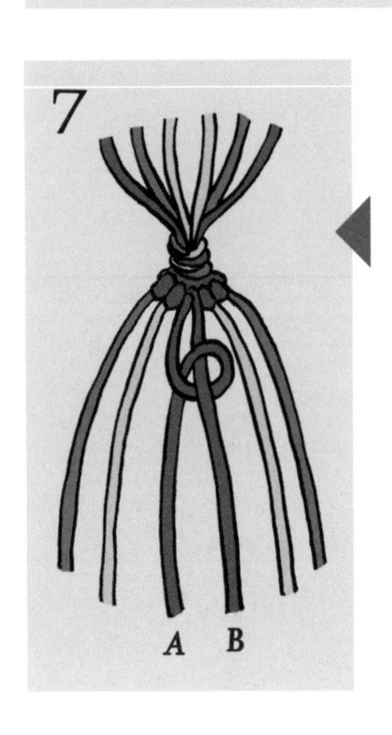

7. Now use purple A to make a reverse knot on purple B.

8. Repeat steps 2–7, using the violet and then the lilac threads to make the knots. Carry on making rows until the bracelet is the length you need, then plait and knot the ends to finish off.

Beautiful as a Butterfly

Colours: Maroon, dark blue, lilac, purple, violet, light blue
Length: One 68 cm length of each colour
Beads: Four silver butterfly beads

This intricate bracelet combines six different colour threads and four delicate silver butterfly beads.

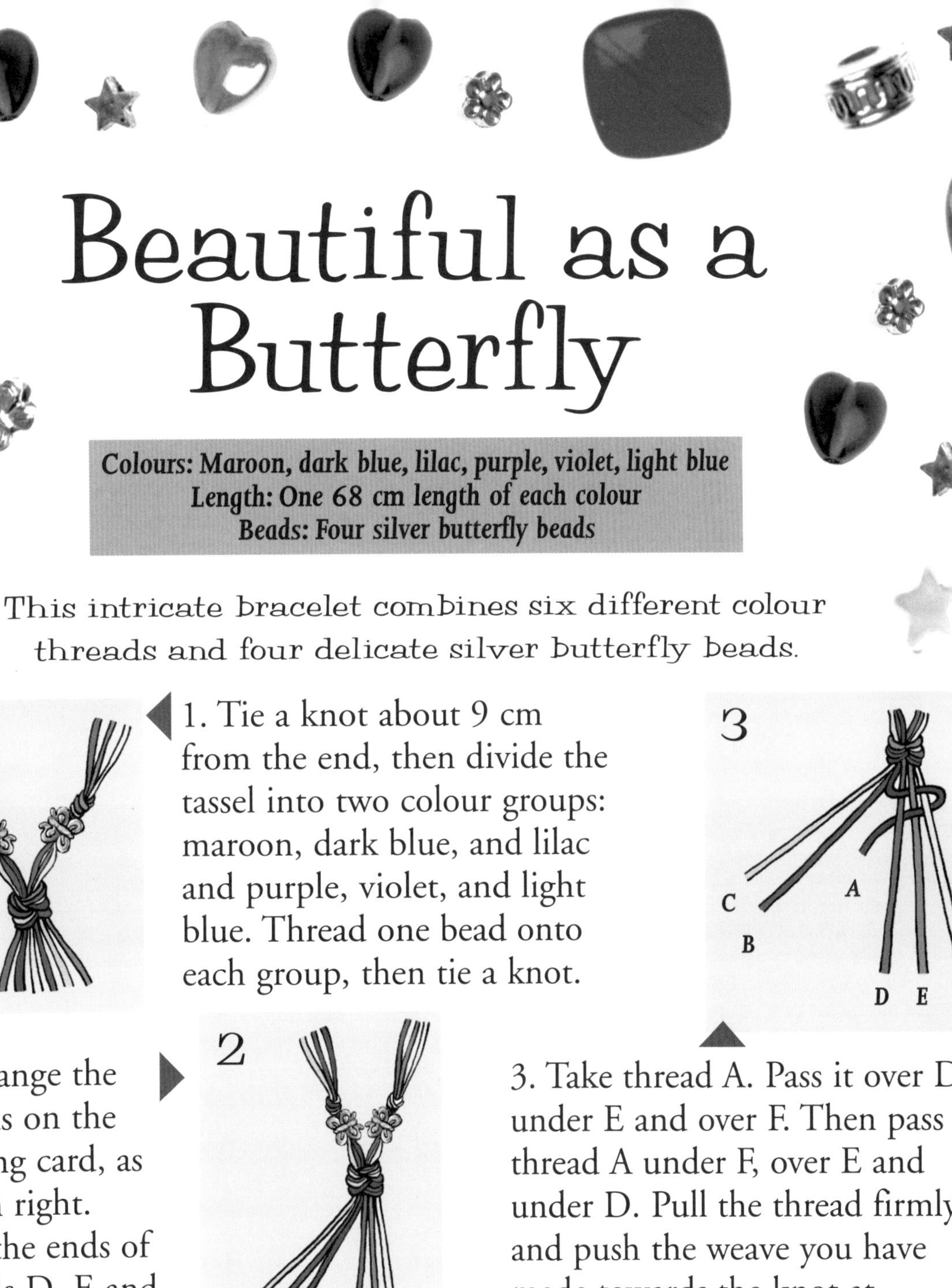

1. Tie a knot about 9 cm from the end, then divide the tassel into two colour groups: maroon, dark blue, and lilac and purple, violet, and light blue. Thread one bead onto each group, then tie a knot.

2. Arrange the threads on the weaving card, as shown right. Tape the ends of threads D, E and F to the weaving card to keep them straight as you weave.

3. Take thread A. Pass it over D, under E and over F. Then pass thread A under F, over E and under D. Pull the thread firmly, and push the weave you have made towards the knot at the top.

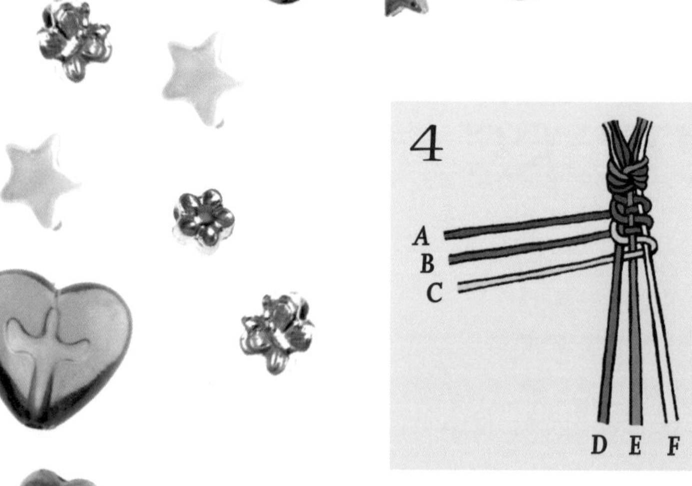

4. Repeat this process using B, then again using C. Push the woven threads neatly and firmly together each time.

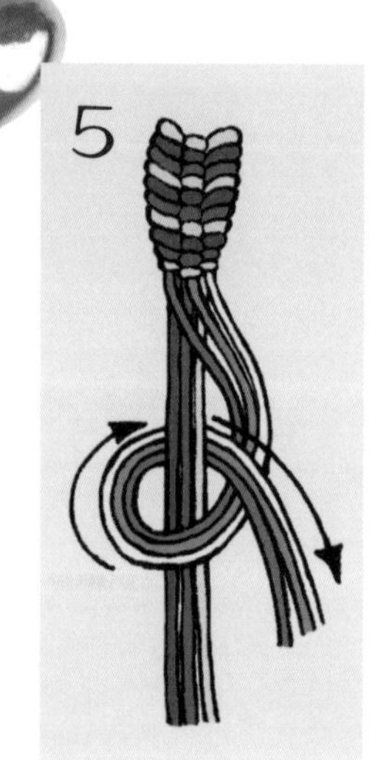

5. Continue weaving with threads A, B and C for $1\frac{1}{2}$ cm. Keeping the threads in their two groups, tie a half knot: pass the right-hand set of threads first over and then under the left-hand threads, then over themselves and back to the right, as shown.

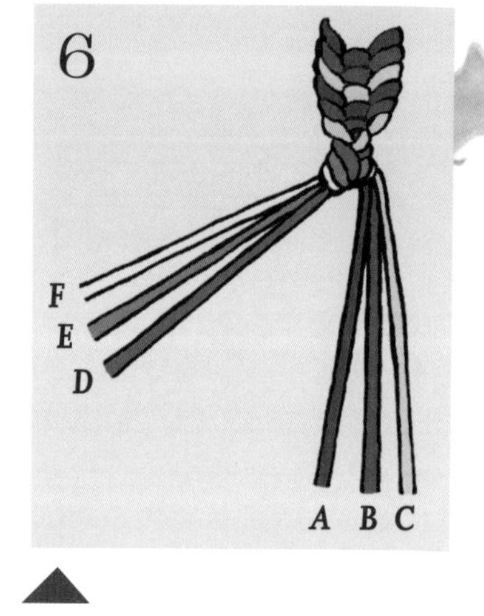

6. Rearrange the threads as shown, so that threads A, B and C are now on the right and D, E and F are on the left.

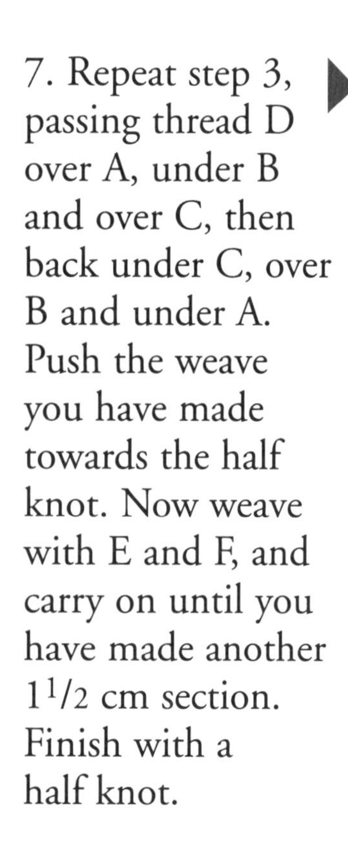

7. Repeat step 3, passing thread D over A, under B and over C, then back under C, over B and under A. Push the weave you have made towards the half knot. Now weave with E and F, and carry on until you have made another $1\frac{1}{2}$ cm section. Finish with a half knot.

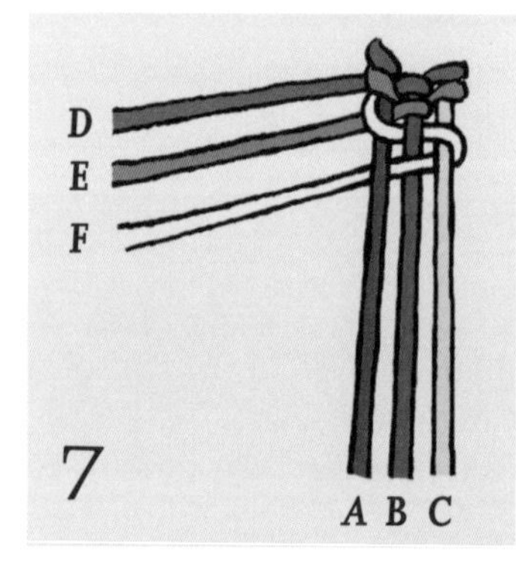

8. Continue weaving, alternating the two colour groups until the bracelet is long enough to go around your wrist, then tie the threads in a full knot. Separate the threads into their two colour groups, thread a butterfly bead onto each tassel and tie a final knot after each bead.

Crisscross

Colours: Pink, lilac, violet, dark blue
Length: Dark blue: two 85 cm lengths; pink, lilac and violet: two 60 cm lengths

If you've worked your way through the other designs in this book, you should be ready to tackle this brilliant bracelet!

This bracelet is more difficult to make as there are more threads to deal with. Take your time when making each knot and try to keep track of which thread is which. You may find it useful to keep a note of the threads, and how many lines you have weaved to refer back to if you get lost. Remember, you can always undo your knots and start again!

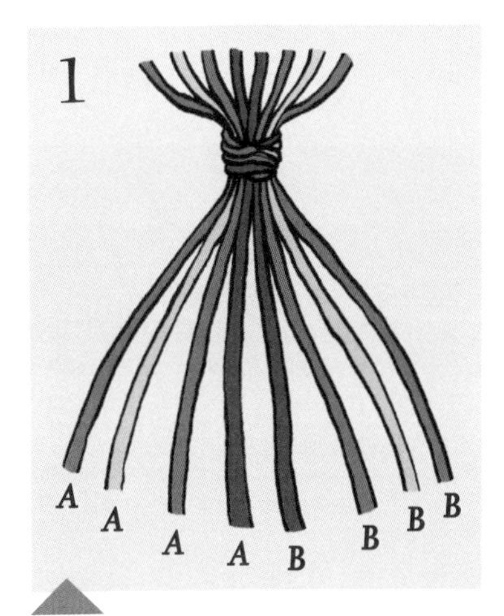

1. Tie the threads together, and arrange them on the weaving card, as shown.

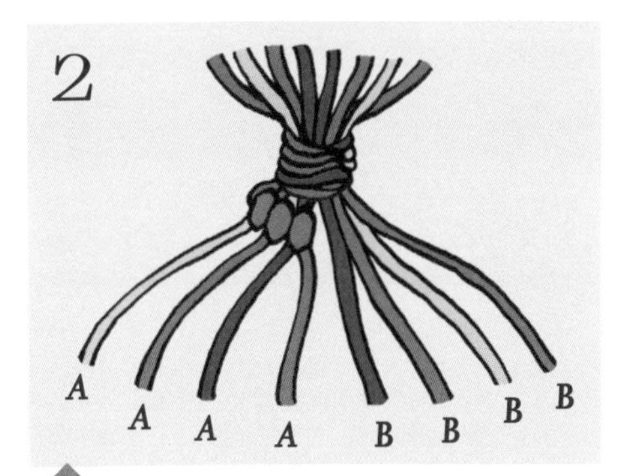

2. Take pink thread A, and make two friendship knots each on threads lilac A, violet A and dark blue A.

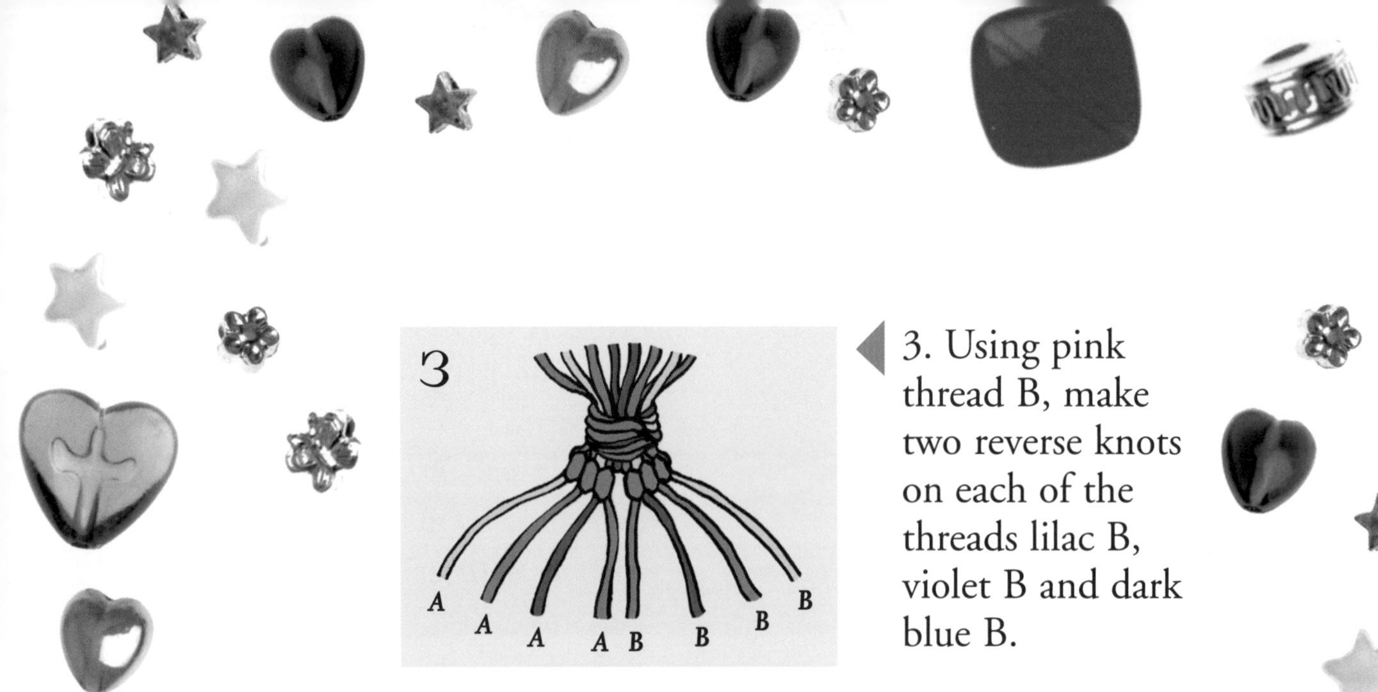

3. Using pink thread B, make two reverse knots on each of the threads lilac B, violet B and dark blue B.

4. Take pink A, and tie one friendship knot and one reverse knot on pink B.

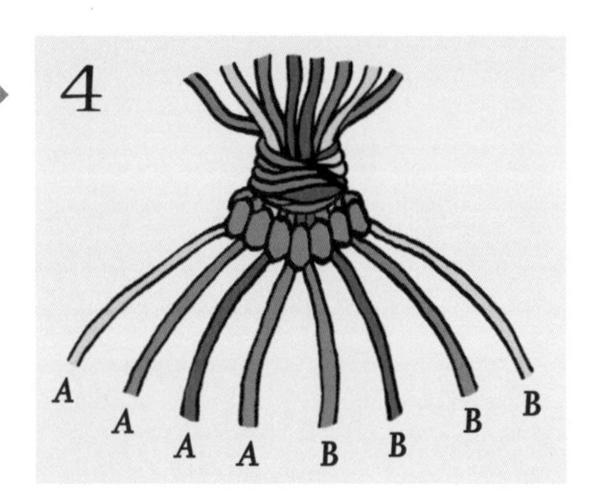

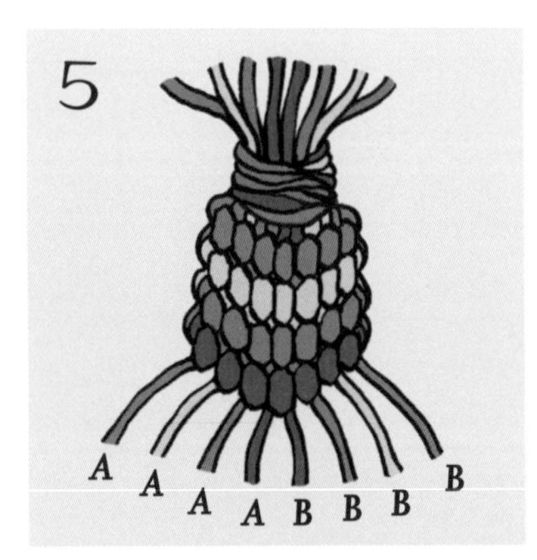

5. Now repeat steps 2–4, this time using the lilac threads to do the knotting. Then repeat the rows with the violet and then the blue threads. (You should end up with the pink threads on the outside again.)

6. Use pink threads A and B to tie another row of friendship and reverse knots on the lilac and violet threads, but not the blue ones.

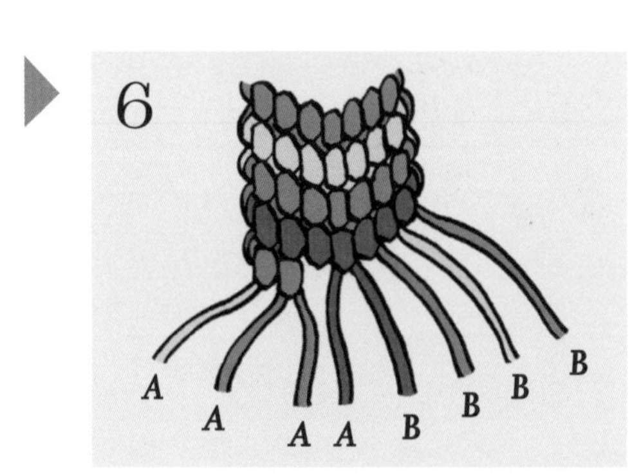

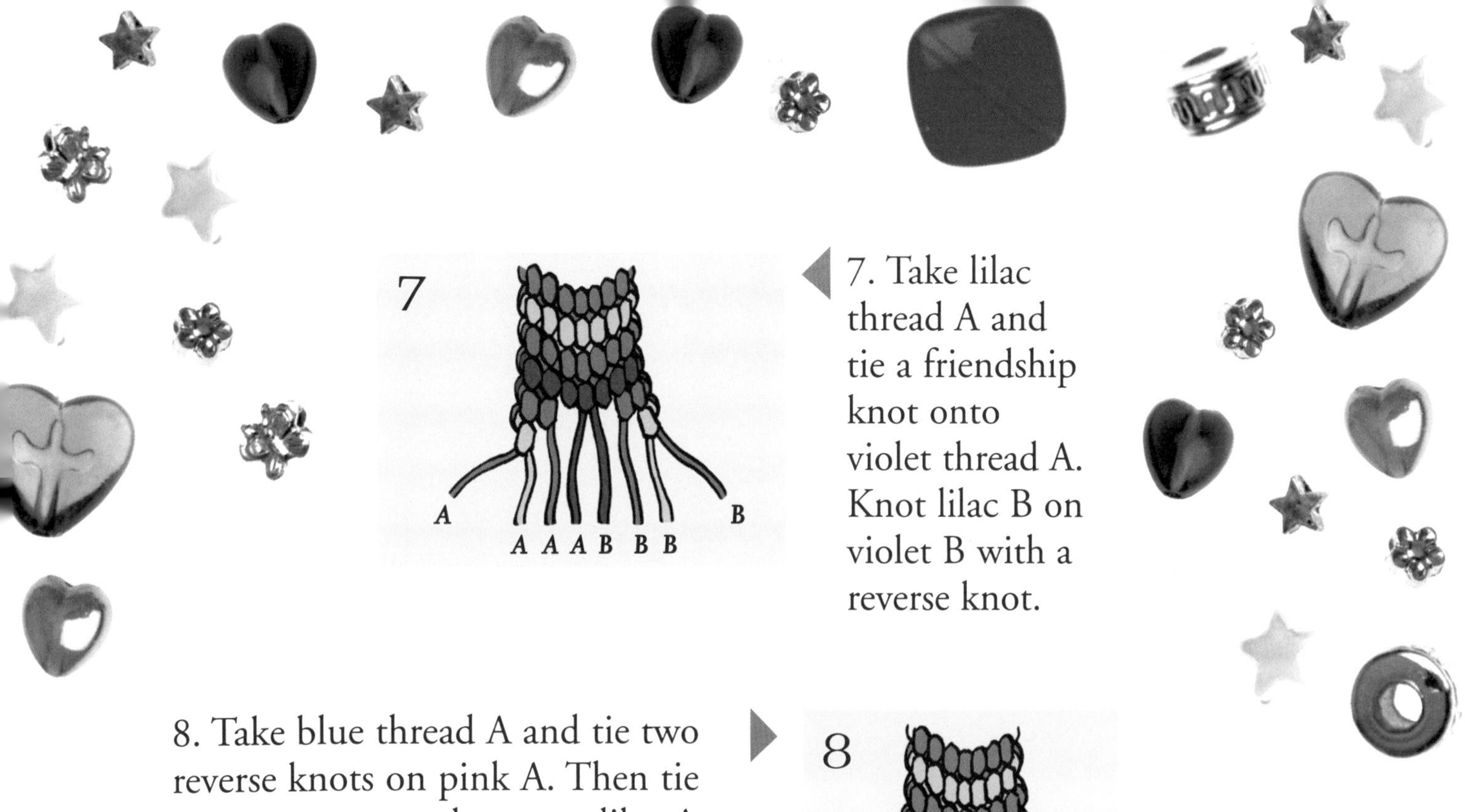

7. Take lilac thread A and tie a friendship knot onto violet thread A. Knot lilac B on violet B with a reverse knot.

8. Take blue thread A and tie two reverse knots on pink A. Then tie two more reverse knots on lilac A and violet A in the same way. Use blue B to tie two friendship knots on pink B, lilac B and violet B.

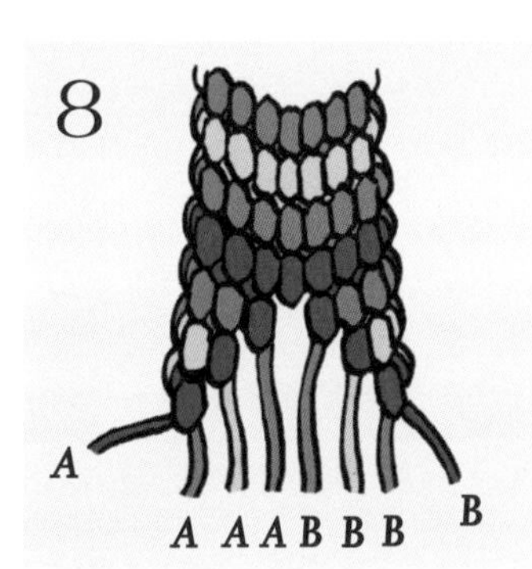

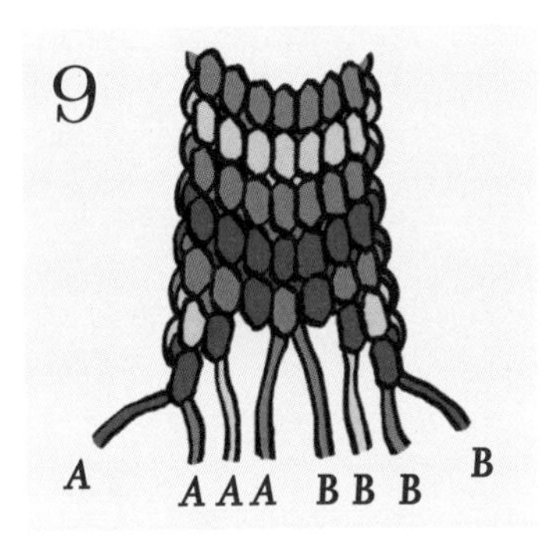

9. Both pink threads are now in the middle. Use pink A to tie one friendship knot then one reverse knot on pink B.

10. Use lilac A to tie two friendship knots on pink A. Then use lilac B to tie two reverse knots on pink B. Now knot the two lilac threads together as you did with the pink threads in step 9.

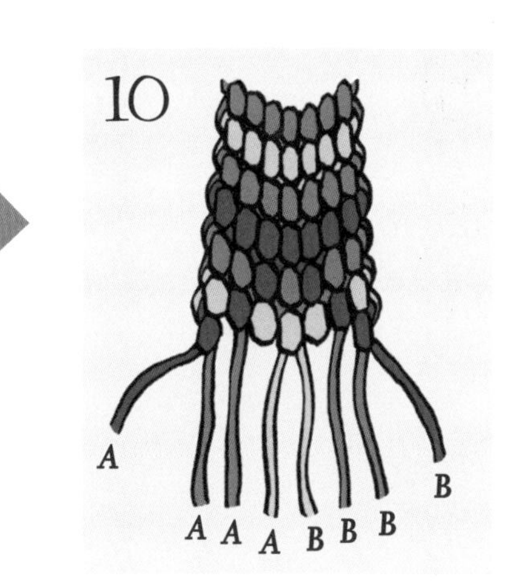

11. Take violet thread A, and tie two friendship knots on pink A and then lilac A. Use violet B to tie two reverse knots on pink B and lilac B. Then tie violet A to violet B, using one friendship knot and one reverse knot.

12. Repeat step 11, using blue thread A to tie two friendship knots on threads pink A, lilac A and violet A, and blue thread B to tie two reverse knots on pink B, lilac B and violet B. Tie blue A to blue B, using one friendship and one reverse knot.

13. Repeat steps 6–12 until you've made seven diamonds. Finish your bracelet by repeating steps 6, 7 and 8, which leaves the pink threads in the middle. Knot the pinks together and out to the edges, then repeat with the lilac and violet threads. Tie the ends as usual.